STRATEGIES FOR SUCCESS:

An Administrator's Guide to Writing

BY DIANE YERKES AND SHARON MORGAN

National Association of Secondary School Principals
Reston, Virginia

About the Authors

Diane Yerkes is associate professor of educational administration at California State University–Fresno. A former English teacher and school and district administrator, she has directed both the successful California School Leadership Academy and the NASSP Assessment Center in San Diego. She also helped develop NASSP's written communications training program, "From the Desk of . . . ."

Sharon Morgan, former journalist, editor, and school public information officer, is currently director of training for the Central Coast Administrator Training Center, a regional office of the California School Leadership Academy. She is also a freelance writer for corporate clients and national magazines, and publishes *Editor-at-Large,* a newsletter service for principals.

Executive Director: Timothy J. Dyer
Associate Executive Director, Editorial Director: Thomas F. Koerner
Editor: Patricia George
Technical Editor: Eugenia Cooper Potter
Publications Specialist: Jody Guarino

Table of Contents

Preface

Nobody ever said writing was easy. It's hard work! Most of us procrastinate—putting off the inevitable—or we struggle to find enough time, choose the right word, or hammer out the perfect piece of writing. Some of us avoid it altogether. But writing is part of every administrator's job.

We have spent nearly a decade reading, critiquing, editing, and helping to improve administrators' writing. We have taught busy people, motivated people, successful people how to be better writers. And, we've learned along the way.

We've learned that some administrators simply need a little support. Others need practice, feedback, and practical tips to make the job easier. Even the most confident writers can use a coach. Thousands of educators have taught us what gets in the way, what makes them reluctant writers, and how tough it is to find the time to write. Extra English classes, how-to books, or computer programs don't seem to be enough.

By using these practical ideas, specific examples, and realistic solutions to the most common writing problems administrators face, we hope you will more easily put thoughts into words.

1 *Writing Basics*

Writing may be hard work, but it need not be painful. Effective writers realize it takes only three special ingredients to write well. Good writers strive to be:

➡ Organized
➡ Clear
➡ Friendly

Be Organized

How we say *what* we say can dramatically affect the impact of our communication. Writing must be organized differently for different purposes. While it is entirely appropriate in a mystery story to save the most important point until last, such an approach is not the best in school communication.

The Inverted Pyramid

Most administrators write for people who need information and prefer it up front and in a clear and understandable form. To fulfill that expectation, the inverted pyramid organization states the most important item first and provides the rest of the information in descending order of importance.

Other Ways To Organize

● *Research Reports.* When reporting on a study of the attendance histories of dropouts or the alignment of the school's curriculum, administrators may use a basic version of the classic research format:
    ✓ State the problem
    ✓ Review literature, facts
    ✓ Explain research methods

✓ State findings, data
✓ Conclude and summarize.

● *Chronological Report.* When reporting on a burglary at the school, principals would probably provide a brief introductory paragraph and then list a step-by-step account of what happened. This approach could also be used to give a brief history of the school, describe the career of a retiring teacher, or prepare a résumé. In the case of a résumé, start with the most recent experiences and work back.

● *Report of an Evaluation Conference.* Most school districts have specific evaluation formats that have been determined by case law, board policy, or administrative procedure. Use the format prescribed by the district. Be careful to use non-judgmental language, support generalizations with specific examples, provide clear descriptions, and give the teacher an opportunity to respond in a timely manner.

● *Persuasive Letter.* Writing to persuade seems to come with the principal-ship. When seeking support, volunteers, money, or someone's time, don't make the request in the first paragraph. Instead, convince readers of the value of the project to them, to their own children, to the future of the community. Then ask, nicely. And leave the readers with specific steps to take: what they are to do, by when, how often, how much, and who else needs to know. And don't forget to convey your appreciation!

Be Clear

Sometimes, without meaning to, we ask our readers to look through windows that are streaked with dirt or splattered with rain. It's hard to "see in." Good writers wash those windows to wipe away the confusion that gets in the way of clear communication.

● *Say it straight.* Don't mince words. Know what you must say and say it. Suppose you have bad news to deliver. Although you will want to "sand-wich" it between positive remarks, you will finally have to say, "We cannot allow the football field to be used for the campout." Don't hedge.

● *Don't be vague.* Children aren't vague. Ask a five-year-old what kind of ice cream he or she wants and you will get a specific answer. "I want chocolate!" Ask an adult what he or she wants for dinner and the answer is apt to be, "I don't care. What do you want?" An explicit response communicates more clearly.

We must be clear in our thinking before we can be clear in our writing. The next time someone asks the perfunctory, "How are you?" answer with a word more precise than "Fine." When writing a letter of recommendation, use specific descriptors rather than broad compliments.

● *Jargon: A Secret Code.* Like professionals in all fields, educators create their own language, relying on words and acronyms unfamiliar to those not working in the field. This jargon is a kind of shorthand useful only to members of the same profession. We cannot expect non-educators to know what terms like "diagnostic assessment," "outcome-based education," "suitable learning environment," or "thinking and meaning-centered curriculum" mean.

Instead of "Join SAC. It meets throughout the year," write: "Parents, students, and staff members are invited to serve on our School Advisory Council (SAC). We meet the first Tuesday evening of every month." It's up to us to translate or define terms that may be unfamiliar to others. No one else will.

● *Avoid Clichés.* Be original. Avoid the overworked words and expressions that have become meaningless in their overuse, such as "Have a nice day!" Most of us hardly hear those words. Phrases like "fall through the cracks," "last but not least," or "thank you for your cooperation" have little meaning and no impact. In your letters:

Instead of . . .	*Use*
the undersigned	I
the above-referenced letter	your letter
enclosed please find	I am sending
attached hereto	included
do not hesitate to call	please call me

Choose your words carefully. Be clear.

Be Friendly

Being friendly also means being reader-centered, positive, open, accepting, sensitive, and warm. The school leader must be all of these. How often do you show your friendliness in what you write?

● *Don't "encourage"* parents to attend a school event. Invite them! How

3

would you ask them to your home for dinner? Would you call? Write a note? How far in advance? Think of community members as your friends. Give them plenty of notice and sufficient details in a friendly invitation. Make them feel that you *want* them to come.

● *Use contractions*. They soften your language and make it more comfortable to read. For example, write, "We're pleased you can join us for College Night," or "It's rewarding to work with students when they're excited about learning."

● *Say it aloud,* as if you were talking to the reader, and then write it that way. People dislike pomposity. Too often, administrators' writing is extremely formal. There's no room or audience for overblown writing on the job. You are a person, an individual with a unique background, interests, and style. Let your readers know the real *you!* Use a friendly tone.

● *Select letterhead,* memo pads, note paper, and cards that reflect your interests, your personality. Hire a graphic artist or ask an artistic friend to commit your professional image to paper. You can also use computer graphics, buy clip art, or try rub-on letters to enhance your written work. Accent what you write with borders and bold headings. Colored paper and ink stand out. Use them when appropriate because **black on white is boring!**

You certainly may represent a school district, so use formal letterhead and a standard format when necessary. But you also represent yourself, an individual with important things to say. Say them with personality!

Why Write?

Writing comes with the territory, but why do we do it? Many of us write:

● To improve our image, both personal and professional
● To avoid misunderstanding, to clarify
● To cover ourselves
● To document
● To explain fully
● To be sensitive
● To model for teachers as well as students
● To avoid procrastination
● To save time
● To make personal connections
● To thank
● To give credit
● To reach busy people despite busy phone lines

4

- To support arguments or positions
- To support other people
- To prevent rumors
- To reflect and to learn through reflection.

And let's face it: there are times we write because we have to!

Writer's Responsibilities

The writer's responsibility is to **communicate the message and make it easy for the reader.**

To do that, the writer must:

- Know the audience
- Choose words the audience understands
- Give them what they want to know, not just what the writer wants to to tell them
- Be sensitive
- Provide names, phone numbers, addresses, other helpful details
- Encourage two-way, open communication
- Be specific
- Be organized, clear, and friendly.

Reader's Rights

Writing is only half of communication. Readers have rights, too. They have the right to:

- Stop reading
- Be offended
- Ignore the message
- Be bored
- Turn the writer's words against him or her.

A well-written message can prevent "reader's revenge."

Making Time for Writing

How do administrators find time to write? Here are some suggestions:

- Schedule an appointment with yourself to write; mark your calendar and keep your appointment.

- Force yourself to make uninterrupted time for creative, difficult, or sensitive projects.
- Have materials such as paper, pen, or resource books handy.
- Know yourself and your work style. Use a computer, dictaphone, lists, notes, clusters, or a yellow pad to assemble your ideas.
- Give yourself lead time; take small steps. Today's notes become tomorrow's head start.
- Write for five minutes every day—on purpose. The hardest part is getting started.
- Leave time for revisions. Everything is a draft until it leaves your office.

Writing for the Occasion

Tuxedo or tennis shoes? Every top-notch professional knows how to dress for the job. It is equally important to choose appropriate words and format to "suit" the occasion as you write. Know your own style and know your audience.

Memo vs. Letter

It would be a waste of your time and your readers' time to develop a five-page letter outlining book return policies when a short memo will do. In this case, teachers want to know what to do, not why they have to do it.

On the other hand, a memo to the president of a chamber of commerce is inappropriate; he or she deserves a letter.

Pen and Paper vs. Machine

Choose the option that your audience will find readable and effective. If your handwriting is illegible, don't write by hand. However, creating a printed page could be a waste of time when the occasion calls for a quick memo. A handwritten proposal or letter of application will appear poorly conceived or hastily prepared. A handwritten thank-you note is always appreciated.

What makes a handwritten note special?

- **It's personal.** The reader knows you have not dictated or dashed it off on-the-run, to be cleaned up later by a secretary. Instead, you have thought about the recipient, found some stationery and a pen, and actually written—in your own hand.
- **It's quick.** Recipients feel good knowing that you spent a few precious moments on them. In fact, you probably *saved* time. If paper, pen, and stamps are readily available, the handwritten note will take far less time

than drafting, dictating, typing, proofing, and correcting. Keep writing supplies handy—in your car, on your desk, in your briefcase—and use them whenever you have a few spare moments.

Formal vs. Informal

Should names in salutations or closings be formal or informal? It depends. In a memo you might address your superintendent as "Jean." In a formal letter the greeting would be "Dear Dr. Murphy." A counselor may be referred to as "Bob" in a staff memo, but as "Mr. Miller" in a letter of termination.

In closing a Welcome-Back-to-School letter to your staff members you can sign "Harriet." A letter inviting parents to Back-to-School Night should be signed "Harriet Williams, Principal." The principal's letter in the student newspaper is usually from "Dr." or "Ms. Williams."

Should you be formal or informal when dealing with sensitive situations? Before you write, consider:

● Your relationship to the *reader*
● Whether you are writing for yourself or on behalf of others
● Whether your letter will be sent to or seen by others, released to the media, or introduced as evidence in a legal proceeding
● Your own style.

Let's Get Personal

Don't be reluctant to get personal. Formality often gets in the way of the relationships we want to build with staff and community. Realizing that communication is a vehicle for building those relationships, it's important, whenever possible, to write in a personal way. One easy technique is to use pronouns to reach out to others.

An example of "impersonal" writing is: *"The administration acknowledges teachers' concerns over after-hours responsibilities but will assign such duties on Wednesday."*

A more effective way to write is: *"We understand that you need a break after a long teaching day. We also recognize that our students must have supervision during school-sponsored activities. Please join us at Wednesday's meeting to choose your after-school assignment!"*

Instead of: *"Members of the administrative staff will host a welcome back meeting for all staff members from 7 to 8 a.m. on September 3 in the cafeteria.—The Administrative Staff,"* write: *"We know you're busy but hope you'll join us for an informal reception in your honor. We'll provide coffee, fruit, and rolls. There is no agenda, no obligation. You simply deserve it! Please come on Thursday, 7:30 to 8:00 a.m., in the library.—Joe."*

Avoid using "the principal" or "the staff." Instead, say "I," as in "I believe that today's schools need . . . ," or "we," as in "We expect good behavior," or "We are determined to eliminate drugs on our campus. . . ."

Use the pronouns "you" and "your," as in the following note to sophomore class leaders: "Congratulations on your successful Orientation Picnic. You have set a positive example for the new freshmen to follow. I'm proud of you." *You* sound like a friendly, caring principal, not the school's supreme ruler!

Writing Right

Principals cannot afford to let poor writing get out the door. It may offend readers, create confusion, and limit the credibility of education as an enterprise, the school as an institution, and the leader as a professional. Consider:

● Creating an editing or reading team that will review each piece of writing that goes to the community. English or business teachers and secretaries can be helpful in catching errors and improving everyone's writing.

● Asking teachers to review each other's writing. The principal should review formal teacher letters home on a regular basis. If teachers aren't writing to parents or students, help them begin to open communication lines.

● Making certain the final copy of any communication (to parents, the board, a teacher, a friend) is correctly written in standard English. Do whatever it takes by

    ✓ Using a dictionary or thesaurus
    ✓ Having a style or usage book on your desk and using it
    ✓ Taking a brush-up course on writing
    ✓ Using a spellcheck, grammar check, or other computer program dealing with writing mechanics. (But don't assume these programs will catch everything!)

2 *Getting Started*

All good writers prewrite. Some make a list; others cluster words and ideas. Many just think about what they want to write. Before you write, consider four key questions:

1. Why are you writing? What is your purpose for writing, what do you want to say and accomplish?

2. Who is your audience? Is it one person or many; what background does the reader have and need to understand your message; what can you leave out; should you send a copy to someone; will this letter be shared or made public?

3. What results do you want? What should the reader think, do, or decide after reading your letter? Are you making a specific "call to action?"

4. What image do you want to project? Are you trying to be helpful, apologetic, objective, caring, confident, appreciative, witty, formal, or informal?

When you know the answers to these four questions you are ready to write.

One good place to begin is to ask some basic questions, the same questions your readers are likely to ask:

- Who?
- What?
- Where?
- Why?
- When?
- How?

9

The writer's job is to answer all these questions as well as to provide any necessary details or facts. Write for the reader who knows less about the subject than you do, but who doesn't want to know everything. These six questions can give you a framework, a place to begin.

Another way to begin is to cluster or brainstorm ideas in your mind or on paper. Start by circling your main idea or purpose in the middle of a blank page.

As ideas, facts, or issues enter your mind, add them in no particular order. Be creative and think big! Now add additional ideas or details, grouping as you go.

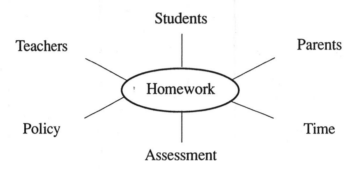

You can process ideas in many other ways. Try to outline, list, write freely without stopping, brainstorm alone or with someone else, sketch concepts, or talk your idea through with a friend. The most important step, however, is to begin.

Getting to the Point . . . Fast

Now take your great ideas, eliminate the not-so-great ideas, and assemble them in readable fashion.

Begin with the most important item first, unless you are sending bad news. Assume that people will only read the first sentence or two; be sure they get your message and are enticed to keep reading.

If, for instance, your school is changing its graduation requirements, you might begin a parent letter like this:

We have something important to discuss with you—your child's education. Join us for a meeting Wednesday to hear about new graduation requirements.

Then provide the additional facts that your readers need in an ordered, logical fashion. You may use the inverted pyramid for organization.

If you have answered the Who, What, Where, Why, When, and How questions in order of importance, then add supporting details. Chances are your readers will have the answers they need.

Writing Tight

A few tricks of the writing trade are worth trying when you want to make your writing more concise. Begin by looking at verbs. Rather than using multiple adjectives and adverbs, use strong verbs. Different verbs carry different messages. You must decide which best convey your point.

Try each of the verbs below in the following sentence. Notice how the meaning changes with each.

The principal will _____ the resources.

channel	distribute
redistribute	define
analyze	find
allocate	acquire

Use the active voice more often than the passive voice. See that your subject takes the action and is not merely acted upon.

Active Voice: **The boy *threw* the ball.**
The coach *reprimanded* the team.
Passive Voice: **The ball *was thrown* by the boy.**
The team *was reprimanded* by the coach.

Notice that the active voice uses fewer words and has more impact.

Use adjectives and adverbs deliberately. They should assist, not dilute, strong nouns and verbs.

Satisfactory: **Parents, upset by what was happening, spoke to board members as well as to the large audience.**

Better: **Angry parents voiced their arguments in the crowded board room.**

And when you've said what you want to say, stop.

Choosing Words Carefully

The main goal of the writer is to be understood. If we don't choose words that are concrete, specific, and in the reader's vocabulary, we fail; our message misses the mark.

Some simple techniques will help:

● When making important points, *illustrate with an example.* Instead of "District tardy policies will be enforced at our schools," tell parents, "If students are tardy four times in one quarter, they will be assigned to a four-hour session at Saturday School."

● *Use metaphors* to make complex concepts concrete. Tell the Rotary Club that, "Football players improve by learning, watching, and practicing a new football play together. Math can be taught in the same way. Students in the classroom can tackle relevant projects with hands-on, practical, cooperative approaches. An integrated approach, in football or in math, enhances learning."

Metaphors link what is already familiar (football) to new concepts (math instruction). They paint a visual, concrete picture for the public.

● *Quantify your concepts.* Rather than describing a student as "active in school and community affairs," write, "George spent three years playing saxophone in the band, volunteered time each week at the hospital, and worked at a local flower shop this past year."

● *Choose words that say exactly what they mean.* If you are vague, readers may misinterpret the message. Instead of telling your staff, "Results will be available *soon,*" write, "Scores will be released *Wednesday* and discussed at *Thursday's* faculty meeting."

By being exact, you've left no room for misinterpretation. Good communication depends on choosing and using the right words.

Taking Out the Garbage

Good writers must be their own best critics. They must be able to analyze what they write and "take out the garbage."

Begin by eliminating unnecessary words. Common and often expendable words include: a, an, the, very, typical, average, good, mostly, and nice. Sometimes these words can be used effectively, but a sentence will often have more impact without them. Notice the difference between this:

"The students worked very hard to make the homecoming parade a big success."

and this:

"Enthusiastic students worked for five weeks to stage a successful and well-attended homecoming parade."

12

Reject redundancies. Ask yourself, "Can one word replace two or more?" Reduce these phrases to one word.

_____	few in number	_____	professional career
_____	end result	_____	summer months
_____	general public	_____	check in the amount of
_____	past experience	_____	joint cooperation
_____	plan ahead	_____	filled to capacity

Be careful not to tell your reader more than he or she needs or wants to know. If you have included superfluous information, delete it. Cover the topic; don't confuse the reader.

Mid-Management Bulge

Children communicate their needs clearly: "I want candy!" Effective executives do the same thing.

Somewhere in the educational process we acquire weighty words and ponderous phrases that cause heavy mid-management bulge. To impress others, we use abstract words and sentences that are long, complex, and pompous. Consider the ways five different people might ask for help:

Child:	Help me.
High School Student:	How am I supposed to do this?
Graduate Student:	The writer requires assistance from outside sources.
Middle Manager:	The organization finds the need to establish an ad hoc committee for the purpose of investigating on-going personnel requirements.
CEO:	I need your help.

Eliminate mid-management bulge in your writing. Pare down your message to be trim and fit—not lightweight, but lean and strong.

3 Writing with Style and Purpose

In the course of the day, administrators may tackle a variety of writing assignments—from short memos to letters of recommendation. Each requires a little different approach to be effective.

Just a Note

Notes are a simple way to share a special thought. They show appreciation and sensitivity . . . that you care, that you noticed, that you're sorry. Just because you work with someone is no reason to lapse into a formal style. Everyone likes a friendly note.

● Make a habit of sending notes—handwritten, on quality paper or cards—to hard-working teachers, a sick student, a parent volunteer, the cafeteria staff, or even your superintendent.

● Keep cards, casual notes, other stationery, and postage stamps handy so it's easy to send a note when the thought occurs.

● Don't make a note of thanks or congratulations more than two or three sentences. Don't spend lots of time describing the action or event. Just write that you noticed and liked what you saw.

● Write promptly. A note received two weeks after an event or accomplish-ment may leave the reader unimpressed. Try to set aside five minutes at the beginning or end of each day to write notes to two or three people. You'll see positive benefits for both writer and reader.

● Make your note stand out. Do something unusual such as using colored ink, writing diagonally across the page, or choosing especially appropriate or clever cards.

● Select two or three styles of notepaper personalized with your initials, the school's logo, or attractive artwork and use them.

Write promptly, positively, and personally.

Breaking Bad News

It's never easy to break bad news, to say no to an applicant, to refuse a teacher request, or to suspend a student. When you have to write a "bad news" letter, do not begin with the most important item first, but rather with a buffer statement that builds a bridge to your reader.

> **Issue:** Student loses sports eligibility because of poor grades.

Buffer: *Earlier this year you and your teammates received our eligibility rules for all school activities.*

Explanation: *We know that you are making efforts to do well in both your academic and sports endeavors.*

Despite the reluctance of some to "get to" the meat of the message, it must be done.

Message: *However, the counseling department has notified us that your current grades make you ineligible to participate as a member of the team for the next three weeks.*

Too often, because of our own guilt, frustration, or anger, this is where most writers stop. Instead, add two more messages: hope and help. If you can sincerely offer suggestions, advice, resources, or "good luck," do it here.

Help: *Tutoring can be arranged each day after school by calling 238-HELP.*

Finally, add an encouraging word if you can.

Hope: *We're anxious to see you back in uniform by January 15.*

By following this formula, you can create a bad news letter in five sentences in five minutes. Then fill in any gaps and the difficult task is completed.

Call to Action

One purpose for writing is to get others to think, act, change, or do something. They won't, unless they know what action to take and what you expect. It's up to you to issue the call to action.

The call could be as simple and informal as "Please give these ideas some thought and let's discuss them over lunch on Thursday." Or it could be as direct as "The budget year concludes on May 1. Please have your purchase requisitions in my office by April 20."

It may be as complex as the recommendations included in a formal evaluation. "As we discussed during your conference, computer skills are a necessity in our office. We will reimburse your tuition at the community college for a three-unit computer class or sponsor you in the district in-service series. Please let me know your plans by January 14."

If you expect a specific result, know what you want and ask for it. Requests unaccompanied by a call to action are merely suggestions.

Room To Respond

Effective communication requires a chance to "talk back." By actively seeking two-way communication you develop a channel for feedback from parents, teachers, and community members.

Try to include room for response in anything you write. It can be simply a name and phone number ("Call Mary Smith at 937-2194 with concerns or compliments!") or a brief survey designed to generate specific information. Your newsletter may include a feedback section complete with lines and your address printed on the reverse side for easy mailing.

For example, when writing a letter to parents proposing new graduation requirements, use only the top half of the page. Provide space in the lower half for parents to share their comments or suggestions. Include your name, phone number, and address as well as a deliberate "invitation" to comment.

Make crucial decisions only after you've given your readers room to respond.

Memos Make It Happen

Notes may be brief and friendly. Reports are usually lengthy documents. Memos, however, are compact communications intended to trigger action.

TO: Our Readers

16

FROM: The Authors
SUBJECT: Tips for Improving Your Memos
DATE: June 18, 1991

1. Memos are a quick call to action. Be sure the reader understands what you want and when you want it.
2. Memos can go up, down, or across the organizational structure. It's all right to send a memo to the boss.
3. Memos are internal business communications. Generally, use letters when writing to people outside the organization.
4. Select the most appropriate format for your message.
   - ✓ Chronological (list of the week's activities)
   - ✓ Analytical (state a problem, your analysis, and solution)
   - ✓ General to specific (most important information first)
5. Keep your audience—not the directive or information—in mind.
6. Always date memos, both for ease in filing and as a courtesy to the reader who may need to respond.
7. Use subject line to define the issue quickly and provide a guide for filing.
8. Make it easy for the reader to take action. Consider adding a contact line: "CONTACT: Call Maryann Jones in Payroll at extension 381."
9. Add a response line at the end. The reader can jot his or her response and send the memo right back to you.
10. Use a printed form if you like. Consider having it printed in script on a half-page to promote brevity and less formal writing. Write in your own hand if it's a quick message.

Begin practicing these tips before the week is over!

"May I Recommend . . ."

Administrators are often asked to write letters of recommendation. Make it easy on yourself.

Before you write, ask for:

- Purpose of the recommendation (the scholarship's requirements or the job's duties)
- Complete and accurate name, title, and address of recipient
- Due date
- Any required forms, file numbers, and a stamped, addressed envelope
- List of accomplishments and goals and a résumé.

When you write:

- Include your title and relationship to the person for whom you're writing.
- Select three or four areas of the candidate's strength and support each

with specific examples.
- Speak to personal as well as professional attributes whenever possible.
- Offer to discuss the candidate's qualifications further and give your phone number.
- Be honest. Don't exaggerate.

After you write:

- Save it. The ideas, language, or examples may be useful again.
- If your letter is positive, consider sending a courtesy copy to the candidate.

Don't:

- Write a glowing, but dishonest, letter in the hopes of moving a "lemon" out of your school.
- Write just because you're asked. Reserve letters of recommendation only for those whose work you know and support. It's appropriate to suggest to anyone asking that the department head or the counselor might give a better recommendation if you are uncomfortable with the request.
- Allow the candidate to review, edit, or write your letter.
- Discuss confidential letters with others.
- Miss deadlines. A person could miss "the big chance."

Apply Yourself

When applying for a position, a scholarship, an administrative award, or a doctoral program, you must *sell* yourself in no more than a page and a half. Sometimes less will do. What should you include?

It depends on two things: who you are and what the announcement or brochure asks for. See that your qualifications "match" the requirements and that your beliefs and values do not conflict with the expectations stated in the announcement.

1. Begin by highlighting key words in the application. "The principal will have a vision . . . commitment to instructional excellence . . . creativity . . . courage . . . a positive attitude . . . energy . . . professionalism, " and so forth.

Next, you might develop an idea cluster with "ME" circled at the center and the key words positioned around it. Add your own qualifications or personal examples that illustrate the key words.

Or, chart the key words and under each, list adjectives that describe you. Add specific experiences to demonstrate your qualifications.

Brainstorm by yourself or with a colleague to generate more ideas.

Try freewriting. Write for a specific time—maybe five minutes—about how you would perform in this position. Loosen up. Visualize your day-today activities and behavior in this job. What do you see yourself doing? How well are you doing it?

2. Next, focus on no more than five or six key areas and organize these in order of importance.

3. Write your letter, incorporating the language of the announcement or application, and give a *few* examples of how you fit the requirements.

4. Reread, revise, and edit.

5. Ask a friend to read your letter and make suggestions.

6. Proofread and revise again until you know your letter is perfect.

Get ready for your interview or award!

4 *Make It Easier, Make It Better*

We can all take a few steps to make the job of writing easier. Try a few of these:

● If you get a letter requiring an informal response, jot your answer on the letter itself and return it to the sender.

● Use the margins of letters as a place to outline your responses. This saves time and ensures that you don't overlook anything important.

● Write once; send twice! Send a letter about short-day schedules to both parents and bus drivers. Notify merchants as well as parents when your "closed" campus approves an "open" lunch policy. There may be no need to write a second memo to a second audience.

● Delegate writing duties to others. Students, staff members, and community members can all write for the school newsletter. Ask the librarian to review a book, a psychologist to discuss peer pressure, or a student to propose solutions to campus vandalism.

● Share good news by sending copies of a complimentary letter to supervisors, teachers, or parents. When someone has something nice to say, ask that it be put in writing. Post fan mail for all to see.

Fan Mail

We all need friends, kind words, a little TLC. If you haven't already, begin collecting positive notes and letters that come your way.

● Refer to them often. Seeing how much others appreciate you is a quick morale booster on bad days.

● Scan fan mail for ideas when giving a compliment, sharing good news, offering praise, or keeping in touch.

● When others on your staff get fan mail, post it in the office, send it to their supervisors, or add a copy to their files. Spread the good news.

Caution: Handle with Care

Effective writers take pains to be accurate, sensitive, and clear. They write with care and with inoffensive words. It's as simple as spelling a name correctly or reaching out to someone in crisis.

● Few things are more personal than an individual's name. Check for accuracy and correct spelling.
● Use appropriate titles. In an address, write "Jane Wilson, Ed. D."; in the salutation, write "Dear Dr. Wilson." If you're not sure about a title, call and ask. If you can't find out, use Mr. or Ms.
● Avoid sexist language. All students are not boys. Use "he" and "she" or write in the plural and use "they." Your employees are entitled to workers' (not workmen's) compensation benefits. Maintenance men are sometimes women, and teachers and administrators come in both sexes.
● Use language appropriate to your audience. Does "chairman" offend the new female board president? Is it better to write, "Committee chairs were named last night"?
● Carefully plan any list of names. Will it be alphabetical? By department? Rank? Seniority? A little forethought may prevent awkward situations and embarrassment.
● Check for omissions. A student is the first to notice if he or she is left off the Honor Roll list. Teachers also feel slighted when their contributions or accomplishments go unrecognized.
● Don't be reluctant to broach painful subjects such as family illness or death, loss of a job, or divorce. Provide support to people in crisis through short notes, cards, or a personal letter. It may be easier to write than to call, but do reach out.

People, Not Programs

People relate to people, not to districts, institutions, or programs. Complex issues can sometimes be illustrated more clearly when seen in one individual's story.

For example, a bilingual program could be chronicled in the reflections of a Vietnamese valedictorian. A discipline procedure could be explained through the misadventures of one hypothetical student. A story explaining the peer counseling program might begin like this:

"Martha DeLany knew that her son was having trouble in school. She was having trouble with him at home. But she didn't know what to do until someone from school called—to help.

It was her child's counselor calling because school officials were also concerned. Teachers had reported dropping grades, truancies, an incident with another student on campus. What Mrs. DeLany discovered was that with the counselor's help she could guide her child to the peer counseling program here at Adams High School. . . ."

Focus your story on a person, not a program.

Check Your References

For the sake of accuracy, we always check facts. But do we check our references?

In education, terms like programs, specialists, or projects are often used without an explanation of *which* program, specialist, or project. If you refer to a conference you would like staff members to attend, make certain you specify which conference, using full name or dates, not acronyms or abbreviations.

When communicating with parents, you may refer to "THEM." Does THEM mean students, teachers, vandals, fathers? This sentence is confusing: "The staff supports PTSA efforts. It pledged funds . . ." *Who* pledged the funds—the staff or PTSA? If we refer to AVERAGE students or AVERAGE grades, do we define AVERAGE? (Remember, to parents, no child is average.)

Check your references. Make sure they are as clear to the reader as they are to the writer.

First and Last Words—Yours

You are the voice of your school. While it may be up to the district to set and communicate policies, only you can speak for your entire school. Your voice must be strong and clear.

● Keep home-school communications a top priority.
● Don't neglect those closest to you. Communicate regularly with staff members formally through bulletins, notices, and announcements, and informally through notes, memos, and personal messages.
● Consider changing traditional staff announcements to a "From Me to You" information sheet. Summarize a current research article, add kudos for staff members who are supporting the school's priorities, and supply facts that clarify concerns or squelch rumors.
● Give students the opportunity to "converse" with you by soliciting student questions about educational, community, or world issues and re-

spond in the school paper.
- Encourage letters from students. Respond in writing.

Decision making is shared by wise leaders. But the first and last words about your school belong to you. Speak up for yourself.

Brag a Bit

If you don't brag, no one will. It's time educators take pride in their profession and use enthusiasm as they deliberately and assertively let others know what's good about our schools. Use writing as an opportunity to share your vision and your dreams for students at the same time you acknowledge the day-to-day success stories.

- Include a success story in every newsletter.
- Begin or end an agenda by sharing one person's success.
- "Sell" a proposal in a letter to the editor.
- Send a positive message on the school marquis.
- Make yourself available as a speaker; ask to be "invited out."
- Write a regular column in the school and community newspapers.
- Work with students to present a radio or television public service announcement.
- Design a bumper sticker that celebrates student success.
- Write thank-you notes for jobs well done.
- Spread your school's motto and mission at every opportunity.

We've been conditioned to do good work quietly. We have believed that "Recognition will come in it's own time." The time is now, and it's up to us to brag a bit.

Putting on the Polish

Polishing is necessary whether we call it revising, editing, or rewriting. Ideally, we provide ample time for each step; sometimes there is none. Whenever possible, reread your work, at least once, as a reader not a writer, as a critic not a friend.

- Help yourself by trying to write in advance of your deadline, so your writing has time to "cool," especially if it's a sensitive memo, an important speech, a "bad news" letter, or a negative performance evaluation. Give yourself and your writing time to rest. When you return to it, it will be easier to see where it could use some polish.

● Look for basic problems in organization, coherence, and clarity. Have you left anything out? Try reading it aloud. Then polish some more by listening closely for compactness, specificity, use of language. Revise as you edit.

● Get a fine shine by proofreading, catching errors in spelling, punctuation, and grammar. If you have a spell check or grammar checking program for your computer, use it. But never trust it! Only knowledgeable human beings, you and someone you trust, can read with eyes, minds, and hearts.

● Know your own weaknesses and try to compensate by relying on a competent secretary or colleague, using handy reference books, and making a conscientious effort to look for errors.

● Save time for yourself and those who provide feedback by adopting a common code of proofreading marks, a shorthand system that makes corrections easy to understand.

● When in doubt, check it out. Make sure dates, times, spelling, and grammar are correct. The time you invest now will pay personal and professional dividends later.

We all act as critics and editors every day when we read writing by others—the morning paper, letters on our desk, or reports from the district office. We know what communicates and what fails to communicate. We need to look at our own work with that same discriminating eye.

Looking Good

You can't deliver your message to an audience you don't have. You must capture the reader's attention before he or she will read what you have written.

Timing is important when communicating with your audience. Consider the calendar before you send out important notices. Will newsletters mailed on the first of the month get lost in a pile of bills? Is three days' notice really sufficient or even polite when inviting parents to school? Should you propose boundary changes a month before school board elections? Time your message carefully.

Can you make your message attractive in some way? Can you headline or title a letter to parents in red ink or larger letters? Is colored paper appropriate? Will a cover sheet on your report make it stand out?

Large blocks of print can discourage readers. Writers must make a conscious effort to:

✓ Vary sentence length to avoid monotony.

24

✓ Use short paragraphs of five to seven sentences.

✓ Present lists of items or complex ideas in easy-to-read form. Use columns, numbers, or bullets.

✓ Feature key ideas by highlighting, boldfacing, underlining, changing the typeface, or indenting. Use white space or borders to set key ideas apart from the body of your text.

PR: Positive Response

What's the payoff for good writing? It's good public relations! As an administrator, you are noticed, listened to, and influential in the lives of many people. You will ensure a positive response by paying a little attention to what and how you write.

What nicer way than a sincere thank you note to praise the custodian, congratulate a student, commend a teacher for an effective lesson, or show appreciation to the parents who hosted your meeting in their home?

What more effective way to reach large audiences than by having a regular, well-designed newsletter mailed to all parents? Reach even greater audiences by writing timely and relevant columns for the local newspaper.

What better way to model that good writing is a cornerstone of clear thinking, good relationships, effective management, and a sound education?

Writing come with every administrator's job. Why not build in the "positive response" that comes from good writing by being a better writer? Begin today!